U.S. Regions

The Natural Environment of the Southeast

Blaine Wiseman

MEDIA ENHANCED BOOKS
AV2 BY WEIGL
ADDED VALUE • AUDIO VISUAL

www.av2books.com

AV² provides enriched content that supplements and complements this book. Weigl's AV² books strive to create inspired learning and engage young minds in a total learning experience.

Your AV² Media Enhanced books come alive with...

Audio
Listen to sections of the book read aloud.

Key Words
Study vocabulary, and complete a matching word activity.

Go to **www.av2books.com**, and enter this book's unique code.

Video
Watch informative video clips.

Quizzes
Test your knowledge.

BOOK CODE

P870376

Embedded Weblinks
Gain additional information for research.

Slide Show
View images and captions, and prepare a presentation.

AV² by Weigl brings you media enhanced books that support active learning.

Try This!
Complete activities and hands-on experiments.

...and much, much more!

Published by AV² by Weigl
350 5th Avenue, 59th Floor
New York, NY 10118

Websites: www.av2books.com   www.weigl.com

Library of Congress Control Number: 2014942117

ISBN 978-1-4896-1234-2 (hardcover)
ISBN 978-1-4896-1235-9 (softcover)
ISBN 978-1-4896-1236-6 (single-user eBook)
ISBN 978-1-4896-1237-3 (multi-user eBook)

Printed in the United States of America in North Mankato, Minnesota
1 2 3 4 5 6 7 8 9 18 17 16 15 14

062014
WEP060614

Project Coordinator: Aaron Carr
Design: Mandy Christiansen

Every reasonable effort has been made to trace ownership and to obtain permission to reprint copyright material. The publishers would be pleased to have any errors or omissions brought to their attention so that they may be corrected in subsequent printings.

Weigl acknowledges Getty Images as its primary image supplier for this title.

Contents

U.S. Regions

The United States is a land with a wide range of animals, plants, natural areas, and **climates**. The country can be divided into five major regions. They are the Northeast, the Southeast, the Midwest, the Southwest, and the West. Each region of the United States has many similarities and differences within it.

Washington

Montana

Oregon

Idaho

Wyoming

Nevada

Utah

Colorado

California

Arizona

New Mexico

Legend

- West (11 states)
- Southwest (5 states)
- Northeast (11 states)
- Southeast (11 states)
- Midwest (12 states)

The Southeast borders three other regions, the Gulf of Mexico, and the Atlantic Ocean.

Pacific Ocean

MEXICO

The Southeast covers 513,263 square miles (1,329,346 square

Alaska

Hawai'i

0   500 Miles

0   500 Kilometers

0   100 Miles

0   100 Kilometers

CANADA

North Dakota

Minnesota

South Dakota

Wisconsin

Lake Superior

Lake Michigan

Lake Huron

Michigan

Lake Ontario

New York

New Hampshire

Vermont

Maine

Massachusetts

Rhode Island

Connecticut

Nebraska

Iowa

Illinois

Indiana

Ohio

Lake Erie

Pennsylvania

New Jersey

Delaware

Maryland

UNITED STATES

Kansas

Missouri

Kentucky

West Virginia

Virginia

North Carolina

Oklahoma

Arkansas

Tennessee

South Carolina

Texas

Mississippi

Alabama

Georgia

Atlantic Ocean

Louisiana

Florida

Gulf of Mexico

N

0   250 Miles

0   250 Kilometers

What Makes the Southeast?

Within the Southeast is a variety of natural areas, waterways, and landscapes. Rolling hills and valleys make up the northern part of the region. The Southeast includes part of the Appalachian Mountains. After the Rocky Mountains, they are the second-longest mountain chain in North America. The Appalachians cut through Virginia, West Virginia, Kentucky, Tennessee, North Carolina, South Carolina, Georgia, and Alabama. In North Carolina, they rise to their highest peak at Mount Mitchell. It measures 6,684 feet (2,037 meters) above sea level, or the height of the ocean's surface.

From the Appalachians, some land slopes down to the coastline. Mighty rivers such as the Mississippi run through many natural **habitats**. The water level in the Mississippi rises and falls, sometimes flooding the flat, low-lying lands around the river. This affects the land and life along the river's route. At the southeastern tip of the United States, Florida juts out into warm waters. The **Gulf** of Mexico is on one side, and the Atlantic Ocean is on the other.

Snowy egrets are common in Florida.

Major Landmarks of the Southeast

In the Southeast, water and stone come together to create landforms. For more than 5,000 years, the Mississippi River has carried soil from the **mainland** United States to the Gulf of Mexico. Mud and sand has built up over time to form a **delta** at the mouth of the river. The Mississippi River Delta is an important **wetland** that makes up about 40 percent of the wetlands on the U.S. mainland. In other parts of the Southeast region, there are caves, mountain ranges, and tall waterfalls.

Louisiana, Mississippi River Delta
The delta extends Louisiana's land 50 miles (80 km) into the Gulf of Mexico. It is made up of different areas called lobes, which take more than 1,000 years to form.

The Great Smoky Mountains form the border between Tennessee and North Carolina. They are part of the Appalachian mountain range.

Florida, Everglades
The Everglades are a series of wetlands in southern Florida that cover 2 million acres (800,000 hectares). That is bigger than the state of Delaware.

Kentucky, Mammoth Cave
For millions of years, rushing water has carved more than 365 miles (587 km) of caves under the hills of Kentucky. Mammoth Cave is the world's longest system of caves.

Georgia, Amicalola Falls
The tallest waterfall east of the Mississippi River is in the southern part of the Appalachian Mountains. The water drops 729 feet (222 m). *Amicalola* means "tumbling waters" in the local Cherokee language.

North Carolina and Tennessee,
Great Smoky Mountains

The Great Smoky Mountains were formed more than **200 million years ago**.

More than **17,000** kinds of plants and animals live in Great Smoky Mountains National Park.

These mountains get their name from the BLUISH HAZE that covers them.

Major Biomes of the Southeast

The Southeast is made up of many different natural areas. However, this region includes only two major land **biomes**. The Southeast has a variety of **aquatic** habitats that support many forms of life. The Everglades and the Mississippi River Delta contain plant and animal **species** that are found nowhere else in the United States.

Mapping the Biomes of the Southeast

Use the map below and the information on the next page to answer the following questions.

1. What is the largest biome?
2. Which state has more than one biome?
3. How many states have a **deciduous** forest biome?

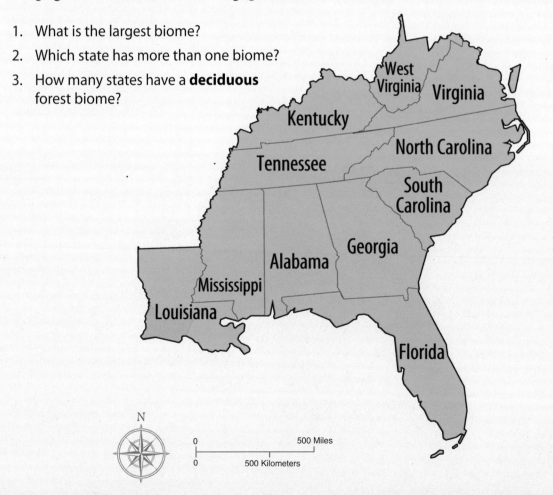

Grasslands

Climate: Dry, seasonal

Vegetation: Grasses

Temperature:
-4° to 86° Fahrenheit

(-20° to 30° Celsius)

Deciduous Forest

Climate: Seasonal

Vegetation: Dense leafy trees, flowers

Temperature: -22° to 86°F

(-30° to 30°C)

In the forests, fields, and bushy areas of the Southeast, the white-tailed deer feeds on leaves and twigs.

Ecosystems of the Southeast

Living things together with their environment create an ecosystem. There are many ecosystems within a biome. They can be large or small. An ecosystem can exist inside a part of another ecosystem. The Everglades make up a large ecosystem. Within the Everglades, the animals and plants in a pond create a smaller ecosystem. Grasslands, forests, mountaintops, caves, wetlands, and oceans support many ecosystems in the Southeast.

Food for Thought

An ecosystem's plants and animals are part of a food cycle. First, plants use energy from sunlight and **nutrients** from the soil to make their own food. Animals called **herbivores** and **omnivores** eat these plants, growing strong from their nutrients. Then, carnivores, or meat-eaters, feed on the plant-eaters. Nutrients in the meat make carnivores grow and thrive. When animals die, they decompose, or break down, over time. The nutrients they gained in life return to the soil, starting the cycle again.

Food Cycle

In a swamp, lily pads begin the food cycle. They collect nutrients from soil below the shallow water.

Fish, such as the sailfin molly, will feed on the lily pads. They gain strength from the plants' nutrients.

An American alligator will get nutrients by eating dozens of sailfin mollies in a single swallow. It passes nutrients to the soil when it dies.

American alligator jaws are **STRONG** enough to **BITE** through turtle shells.

Great Smoky Mountain National Park is the Salamander Capital of the World.

The Southeast is home to the Venus flytrap plant, which eats insects.

The Southeast's alligator gar fish weighs up to **300 pounds** (140 kilograms). Its long snout is filled with **RAZOR-SHARP** teeth.

In 2013, a **NEW** shark species, the Carolina hammerhead, was discovered off the coast of South Carolina.

Major Rivers of the Southeast

In the Southeast, a ridge called the Eastern Continental Divide runs along the top of the Appalachian Mountains. Rivers on the east side flow into the Atlantic Ocean. Rivers on the west side empty into the Gulf of Mexico. All these waterways have helped shape the land. They create huge canyons, lakes, and many other landforms in the region. These rivers also influence the animal and plant life. The longest river in North America is the Mississippi.

Louisiana, Mississippi River
The Mississippi River runs 2,340 miles (3,766 km) from Minnesota to the Gulf of Mexico. With its **tributaries**, it drains, or collects water from, 1.2 million square miles (3.1 million sq. km) of land.

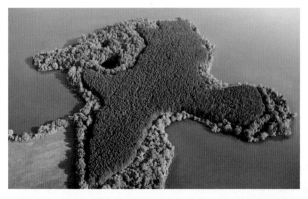

Tennessee, Tennessee River
From its start in Tennessee, this river flows 886 miles (1,426 km). It bends into Alabama before curving back through Tennessee to Kentucky. It flows into the Ohio River, which then empties into the Mississippi.

Georgia, Chattahoochee River
Flowing 436 miles (702 km), the Chattahoochee forms part of the borders between Georgia and Alabama, and Georgia and Florida. In Florida, it joins with the Flint River to create the Apalachicola River.

Georgia and South Carolina, Savannah River
The Seneca and Tugaloo Rivers come together in Georgia to form the 314 mile (505 km) Savannah River. The Savannah forms the boundary between Georgia and South Carolina before emptying into the Atlantic Ocean.

Alabama, Mobile River
The Mobile River is only 45 miles (72 km) long, but it is part of a much larger river system. With its tributaries, the Mobile drains an area of 44,000 square miles (114,000 sq. km). That is larger than the state of Tennessee.

Mammals of the Southeast

With so many different habitats throughout the Southeast, the region is home to a variety of **mammals**. From the peaks of the Great Smoky Mountains to the depths of the Gulf of Mexico, mammals play an important role in Southeast ecosystems. **Endangered** marine, or sea, mammals in the region include right whales and Florida manatees.

Mississippi, Bottlenose Dolphin

Bottlenose dolphins are one of the world's smartest animals. Each dolphin has its own signature whistle, or call. Dolphins also use body language, such as head shaking or hand signals, to communicate.

Georgia, Right Whale

Right whales live in coastal waters. Humans have hunted these whales for hundreds of years. Their parts have been used for lamps, umbrellas, and hairbrushes.

South Carolina, White-tailed Deer

White-tailed deer are the smallest member of the deer family in North America. To escape **predators**, they can jump as high as 10 feet (3 m) and as far as 30 feet (9 m).

Tennessee, Raccoon

The word *raccoon* comes from the Algonquian word for "he who scratches with his hands." Raccoons eat fruits, plants, frogs, and insects.

Virginia, Virginia Big-eared Bat

The Virginia big-eared bat lives in caves all year, **hibernating** in the winter. This endangered species feeds on moths and other insects.

Kentucky and North Carolina,
Eastern Gray Squirrel

Eastern gray squirrels live in trees all over the Southeast. They hide seeds and nuts in their dens, or homes. This food source is useful during winter when food is hard to find.

Florida, Florida Panther

Florida panthers are a type of cougar. These cats used to live all over the Southeast and other parts of the United States. Today, they are an endangered species.

Alabama, Louisiana, and West Virginia,
Black Bear

Black bears are omnivores that mostly eat plants. The Louisiana black bear is its own **subspecies**. This subspecies has longer, narrower skulls than other black bears.

f the South

Reptiles and Amphibians of the Southeast

The Southeast provides perfect habitats for a variety of reptiles and amphibians. Many of these **cold-blooded** animals are found near lakes, streams, swamps, and coastal areas. Others live far from water sources, burrowing into wet soil. Reptiles are more common away from water. They lay their eggs or give birth on land. Snakes, lizards, and crocodiles are reptiles. Amphibians lay their eggs in or near water. Young amphibians, such as tadpoles, live in the water, breathing through **gills**. As they get older, they grow lungs and move to the land. Frogs and salamanders are amphibians.

Florida is the **only place** in the United States that is home to alligators and crocodiles.

Eastern box turtles can live for **more than 100 years**.

Official State Amphibians

Alabama, Red Hills Salamander		The Red Hills salamander lives in a 50-acre (20-ha) area of Alabama. Human activity in this area has reduced the population of this endangered animal.
Georgia and Louisiana, American Green Tree Frog		Green tree frogs live in swamps and marshes all over the Southeast. They hunt insects in the sunny areas of their habitat.
Tennessee, Tennessee Cave Salamander		The Tennessee cave salamander lives in streams inside caves. It never moves to the land and has three large feathery gills for its entire life.

Official State Reptiles

West Virginia,
Timber Rattlesnake

Timber rattlesnakes are venomous snakes that blend in with leafy forest floors. Rattlesnakes shake a bony rattle on their tail when they are in danger.

Alabama,
Alabama Red-bellied Turtle

Red bellies live in the waters of the Mobile Delta. They can live as long as 50 years in nature.

South Carolina,
Loggerhead Sea Turtle

Loggerheads are the largest hard-shelled turtles in the world. They can be 3 feet (1 m) long and weigh up to 1,000 pounds (450 kg).

Georgia,
Gopher Tortoise

Gopher tortoises have roamed the Southeast for 60 million years. This endangered species digs burrows that are shared with animals such as rabbits and armadillos.

Florida, Louisiana, and Mississippi,
American Alligator

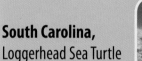

American alligators live in wetlands and swamp areas, digging holes for shelter. When these holes fill with water, they create small ecosystems with fish, insects, plants, and other reptiles.

Tennessee and North Carolina,
Eastern Box Turtle

Eastern box turtles are omnivores that live in forests and meadows throughout the Southeast. Females usually have yellow eyes, while the males' eyes are red.

Unofficial State Reptile

Louisiana,
Copperhead

Copperheads are found in many habitats throughout the Southeast. In different parts of the region, these snakes live in forests, on rocky mountainsides, or near swamps.

Birds of the Southeast

Birds play an important role in ecosystems all over the Southeast. They are a large part of the food cycle wherever they live. Some species eat plants, and others eat meat. Birds may be eaten by other animals. Huge numbers of birds live in the Southeast. Great Smoky Mountains National Park is home to about 240 bird species. About 350 types of birds live in Everglades National Park. Throughout the year, the Mississippi River Delta supports 100 million birds.

Alabama, Yellowhammer
The yellowhammer is a woodpecker. Instead of tapping on tree trunks to find insects in the bark, it looks for bugs and berries on the ground. It is not as strong as most other woodpeckers, preferring to peck soft surfaces.

Brown pelicans dive straight down into the water from high in the air to hunt fish.

Female brown-headed cowbirds lay eggs in the nests of more than 220 bird species. Those birds often then raise the young cowbirds.

Wood duck ducklings can safely jump from nests almost 300 feet (90 m) high.

Florida, Mississippi, and Tennessee,
Northern Mockingbird
Mockingbirds can sing up to 200 songs. They mimic, or mock, the sounds they hear in their environment.

Louisiana, Brown Pelican
In the 1960s, as a result of **pollution**, Louisiana had no brown pelicans. However, the birds have recovered. Today, about 40,000 live in Louisiana, which is known as the Pelican State.

Kentucky, North Carolina, West Virginia, and Virginia, Cardinal

Female cardinals are brown, while males are bright red. The males protect their territory and sometimes attack small red objects thinking they are other cardinals.

Georgia, Brown Thrasher

Brown thrashers sing loudly from shrubs and treetops. These birds offer more than 1,000 types of song.

South Carolina, Carolina Wren

Carolina wrens live in large numbers all over the Southeast. They move quickly along the ground, or up and down tree trunks, looking for food.

Cardinals sometimes attack their own reflection because they think it is another bird.

Woodpeckers "drum" on objects with their beaks to communicate.

A single pair of bobwhite quail can produce up to 25 babies in one mating season.

Tennessee and Georgia, Bobwhite Quail

The bobwhite quail is the official **game bird** of Tennessee and Georgia. Its name comes from the mating call of the males, which sounds like "bobwhite."

Mississippi, Wood Duck

The wood duck is the official state waterfowl of Mississippi. The brightly colored bird is one of the few ducks that perches on branches.

Plants of the Southeast

Plants are a key part of Southeast ecosystems. Trees, shrubs, and flowers provide food and shelter for many animals in their ecosystems. In wetlands, such as the Mississippi River Delta and the Everglades, plants act as a water filter, trapping and blocking pollution. American chaffseed and Louisiana quillwort are endangered plant species in this region.

Alabama
Camellia is a flower that was introduced to the Southeast. It is **native** to China, Japan, Korea, and Taiwan. Camellia replaced the goldenrod as Alabama's state flower in 1959.

A passionflower vine can grow more than 25 feet (8 m) long.

The early U.S. Navy ship called the USS Constitution was built with live oak wood.

Kentucky
Goldenrod is one of the most common wildflowers in the United States. About 30 different types of goldenrod grow in Kentucky.

Louisiana and Mississippi
Magnolia blossoms are common in the Southeast, especially in gardens. The magnolia blossom has been the official flower of Louisiana since 1900 and of Mississippi since 1952.

South Carolina
Yellow jessamine grows naturally in every part of South Carolina. These flowers are the first to appear in spring. They grow on vines that climb trees and fence posts.

Tennessee
Passionflower is a purple flower that grows throughout the Southeast. It is also known as the wild apricot or the maypop. Its American Indian name is Ocoee.

North Carolina and Virginia
Dogwood flowers are usually white or pink early in the season. They blossom on trees that are 20 to 40 feet (6 to 12 m) tall.

It can be deadly to eat the poisonous yellow jessamine.

Dogwood "berries" are actually a type of fruit called drupes, similar to plums.

West Virginia
Rhododendron flowers come in many colors. However, the word *rhododendron* comes from the Greek for "red tree." There are 850 species of rhododendron in the world.

Florida
Orange blossom is Florida's official flower. The orange is the state fruit, and orange is the state tree.

Georgia
Live oak is often wider than it is high. The thick, heavy branches cover a large area and serve as natural protection from hurricanes.

Challenges Facing the Southeast

Natural areas all over the Southeast face many challenges. Wetlands, coastlines, and grasslands are some of the world's most sensitive ecosystems. Large numbers of people live in or near these natural areas. Human activity continues to affect the ability of plants and animals to survive in their natural habitats. Some people and organizations are working to protect these ecosystems from being damaged or disappearing. These groups are addressing issues related to pollution, **climate change**, and expanding human populations.

Deltas, such as the Mississippi River Delta, act as barriers to severe weather, such as hurricanes.

Human Impact

Many dams and **levees** control the flow of the Mississippi River system. These human-made structures stop soil from reaching the Mississippi River Delta. Less soil buildup increases the risk of flooding. Waste from cities and oil spills in the Gulf of Mexico also cause damaging pollution. In addition, climate change is causing water levels in the Gulf, and around the world, to rise. The Mississippi River Delta is one of the natural areas at greatest risk anywhere in the world. Some experts say it could disappear in fewer than 100 years.

In 2005, Hurricane Katrina struck the Southeast, crashing through levees and flooding New Orleans, Louisiana. Since then, the levees have been rebuilt.

Mississippi River Delta

An area about the size of a football field is lost in the Delta every **30** minutes.

The Mississippi and Central Flyways, two major bird ROUTES, come together at the Delta.

The **LARGEST** offshore oil spill in history took place near the coast of Louisiana in 2010.

Endangered Species Spotlight

The Florida panther is the only type of cougar left in the Southeast. Panthers live in habitats such as the swamps, **tropical** forests, and prairies of southern Florida. They roam in areas as large as 200 square miles (500 sq. km). Much of their habitat has been lost as people build communities and convert natural areas to farmland. Today, there are fewer than 200 Florida panthers left in nature.

Manatees are large mammals that live in shallow waters such as swamps, rivers, and coastal areas. Sometimes called sea cows, these plant-eating animals can weigh up to 1,300 pounds (600 kg) and grow to 13 feet (4 m) long. Manatees are slow swimmers that stay close to the surface of the water. Dangers include motorboats and fishing nets in their habitat.

Right whales can grow to 50 feet (15 m) long and weigh 70 tons (64 tonnes). They can live for 100 years.

The right whale got its name because, in the past, people thought it was the "right" whale to hunt. Swimming slowly near the surface, these giants of the sea were easy to find and capture. They have a large amount of **blubber**, which was used for oil and other products. Today, northern right whales are the rarest species of large whale in the world. Fewer than 1,000 of them remain.

One road in Florida has a lower speed limit at night to protect Florida panthers from cars.

Get Involved

The Florida panther is one of the world's most endangered mammals. Threats include hunting, loss of habitat, car strikes, and disease. Protecting their habitat is key to saving the panthers. The U.S. government has created a protected area for Florida panthers to live in. One way you can help is by asking government leaders to do more for endangered species such as the Florida panther.

You can get involved in efforts to save the Florida panther. The website of the Friends of the Florida Panther Refuge offers detailed information about these animals, including what challenges they face, what the latest news is, and how you can help.

For more information, visit the Friends of the Florida Panther Refuge at http://floridapanther.org.

Activity

Burmese pythons can live for 25 years. They grow to be 25 feet (8 m) long and weigh up to 400 pounds (180 kg). These large snakes are native to the jungles of Southeast Asia. They were first brought to the United States because they were popular as pets. However, when the snakes grow large, some careless owners have released them into nature.

Roaming free in the Everglades, Burmese pythons hunt and eat native animals. They also take food sources from native species. There are few predators in this ecosystem. The Burmese python is considered an **invasive species**. More than 1,800 Burmese pythons have been removed from Everglades National Park.

Burmese pythons eat a variety of animals, from small birds to alligators.

Make a Food Web

Use this book, and research on the internet, to see how an invasive species affects an ecosystem.

1. Make a food web of the Everglades, with the American alligator at the top. A food web is made up of connected food chains.

2. Find out what kinds of animals this predator eats, and add them to the web.

3. Continue building the food web, thinking about the relationships between each animal and the food it eats.

4. Now add the Burmese python to your food web.

5. Research the animals that this python eats.

6. Write down the effect this invasive species has on each of the other species in your food web. Share the results with your class, friends, and family.

Sample Food Web

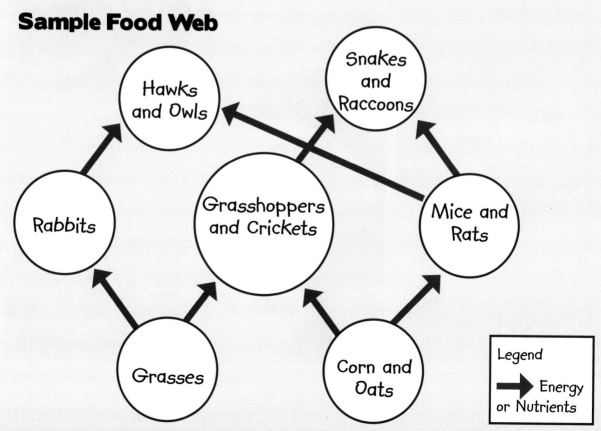

Legend
→ Energy or Nutrients

Quiz

1 What is the highest peak in the Appalachians?

2 What is the world's longest cave system?

3 Which national park is the Salamander Capital of the World?

4 In what state is the Mobile River?

5 What is the largest hard-shelled turtle in the world?

6 What type of fruit are dogwood berries?

7 How many brown pelicans live in Louisiana?

9 What animal is also known as the sea cow?

10 Burmese pythons are considered what kind of species in Florida?

8 Which two flyways come together at the Mississippi River Delta?

ANSWERS: 1. Mount Mitchell 2. Mammoth Cave 3. Great Smoky Mountains National Park 4. Alabama 5. Loggerhead sea turtle 6. Drupes 7. About 40,000 8. The Mississippi and Central Flyways 9. Manatee 10. Invasive

Key Words

aquatic: related to water

biomes: large communities defined by their climate, plants, and animals

blubber: a layer of fat in some sea mammals such as whales and seals

climate change: a change in average temperatures and other weather conditions over a long period of time, such as the warming trend that most scientists believe has been taking place over the past century

climates: usual weather conditions of regions

cold-blooded: having a body temperature that changes with the environment's temperature

deciduous: losing leaves each winter

delta: an area at the mouth of a river where sand and mud builds up

endangered: at risk of no longer surviving on Earth or in a particular region

game bird: a bird that can be hunted

gills: organs that fish and amphibians use to breathe

gulf: a part of an ocean or sea that is partly surrounded by land

habitats: the places where an animal or plant naturally lives

herbivores: animals that feeds mainly on plants

hibernating: spending the winter in an inactive state

invasive species: a species that harms an ecosystem to which it is not native

levees: banks built along a river to keep it from overflowing

mainland: the main part of an area, such as the United States without Alaska and Hawai'i

mammals: animals that have hair or fur and drink milk from their mother

native: originating and growing in a certain place

nutrients: substances that living things need to survive and grow

omnivores: animals that eat plants and animals

pollution: harmful substances that are put into the environment

predators: animals that hunt other animals for food

species: a group of similar animals or plants

subspecies: a subdivision of a species, usually in a separate area

tributaries: small rivers that flow into larger rivers

tropical: hot and humid

wetland: lowland area wholly or partly covered with water

Index

Log on to www.av2books.com

AV² by Weigl brings you media enhanced books that support active learning. Go to www.av2books.com, and enter the special code found on page 2 of this book. You will gain access to enriched and enhanced content that supplements and complements this book. Content includes video, audio, weblinks, quizzes, a slide show, and activities.

AV² Online Navigation

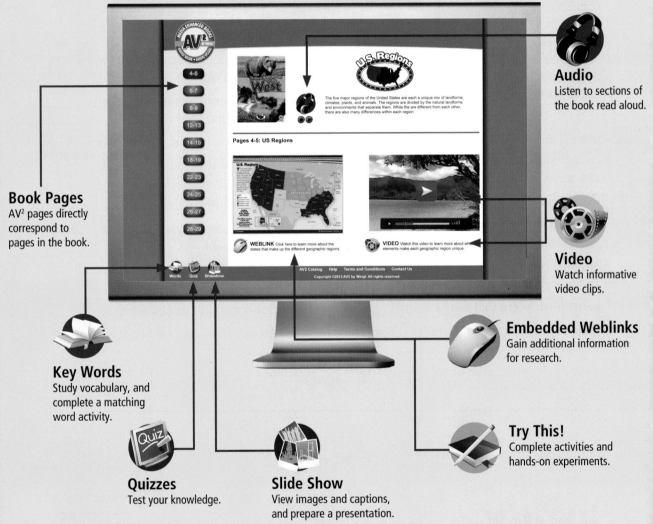

Audio
Listen to sections of the book read aloud.

Video
Watch informative video clips.

Embedded Weblinks
Gain additional information for research.

Try This!
Complete activities and hands-on experiments.

Slide Show
View images and captions, and prepare a presentation.

Quizzes
Test your knowledge.

Key Words
Study vocabulary, and complete a matching word activity.

Book Pages
AV² pages directly correspond to pages in the book.

AV² was built to bridge the gap between print and digital. We encourage you to tell us what you like and what you want to see in the future.

Sign up to be an AV² Ambassador at www.av2books.com/ambassador.